AF240879

Understanding Feminism

Comprendre/Essai graphique
a collection directed by Luis de Miranda
Max Milo éditions, Paris, 2023
www.maxmilo.com
ISBN 978-2-315-01258-9

Marie-Hélène Bourcier
Alice Moliner

Understanding Feminism

Max Milo

COMPRENDRE/ESSAI GRAPHIQUE

In the car, Simone,
we're the ones who honk!

1.

Who are they? The "we" of Feminism

"Don't set me free, I'll take care of it!"

FEMINIST SLOGAN

WHAT IS FEMINISM? A vast question, often answered by a battery of dates or a controversial history. This 100-page tour de piste takes a different approach. Understanding feminism also means looking at the problems it poses and is posing. Its toolbox, its mutations and contradictions, its limits and resources, the objectives of a major political and cultural revolution underway since the 19th century. To its way of making the subject, politics, culture, art, cinema, the media, of fabricating femininity and masculinity. Changing gender and the relationship to knowledge. To gentrify, soften or frighten. To have changed the lives of thousands of women and failed to convince many more. To be divided.

You're not born a feminist, you become one. This little book focuses on those who have become feminists, without privileging the best-known. To understand feminism is to be part of its currents, scenarios and debates. And to start with, let's ask ourselves a different question from that of defining feminism: who's doing what today? Who are the feminists?

But it's obvious! Feminists are women who fight for other women and identify with all those who suffer patriarchal oppression or male domination. Yet this feminist "we" is far from self-evident. Its composition, its claims to represent women in a totalizing way - these are all vexing issues at the heart of contemporary feminist debates. It's even THE question posed by third-wave feminism (in the 1990s) to first- and second-wave feminisms (the suffragettes of the 19th century and the **MLF** of the 1970s).

VOTES FOR WOMEN

LES TROIS VAGUES DU FÉMINISME

How can we "dehomogenize" this feminist "we" that has proved so exclusionary?

Failing to include them politically, white feminists in the West had to listen to the black feminists who had been protesting since the 1970s in the United States. Not to mention the Chicano feminists and many others who pounded their fists on the table. Their feminism took into account the specificity of their oppression. It also emphasized the fact that "white middle-class" feminists could participate in it, and even reinforce it. In fact, oppressions linked to race, class, age, ability, gender and sexuality are intertwined (known as "intersectionality"). It is therefore abusive to hierarchize them by making them derive from patriarchal oppression, as if this were matrix or transhistorical. As if the others came after, as if they were less important.

Using slavery as a metaphor for the oppression of women, for example, is a tenacious Eurocentric and racist habit in white feminism. Like the way racism is brought back into debates on male/female inequality in today's France, to imply that it would be more indisputable, easier to denounce or even... more "visible". Racism: the darling of discrimination? Better understood or less tolerated than sexism? In these so-called "post-colonial" and very post-9/11 times, isn't the question rather to ask how feminism can avoid replaying the colonialist card of rescuing the veiled woman from her violent, rapist, Arab husband? Not to erase the Muslim and Islamic feminists whose existence we are only just beginning to recognize, and to admit that neither modernity nor feminism are exclusive to the Western world?

As you can see, the current challenge for feminism is to reduce its exclusionary effects. Some people take offence at this criticism and take refuge in feminist sentiments. And yet, feminism is big enough to admit that it must ward off its Eurocentrism and its class point of view. By failing to do so, it runs the risk of freezing and promoting an ethereal, essentialized vision of women, which cuts it off, whether deliberately or not, from women in all their diversity and complexity. All the more so as it also has a hard time breaking with its heterocentric vision, despite the fact that its linchpins have often been lesbian feminists. Less directly involved in the struggle for abortion or the pill, they nevertheless spared no effort from the 1970s onwards. But no political recognition. How cramped they felt in a feminism identified as "woman", which hardly corresponded to their expression of masculine gender (with butch lesbians[1]), or borrowed from other registers of femininity! Far from representing splintered minority demands, lesbian feminism, lesbian feminists, transsexuals or transgender feminists, and queer feminism show us just how dependent feminism is on its definition of woman and femininity, and its conception of "sexual difference".

So what is this standard of sexual difference that we are constantly reminded of by the signage on toilet doors? Two doors, two sexes, two genders.

---

1. The term "empowerment" refers to lesbians who have assumed masculine gender expression. The term can also refer to forms of gay masculinity.

LA
FEMME

Why is it at the heart of every feminist scenario? To summarize. For both men and women, there's an infallible continuity between their biological sex and their gender. A female sex, female genitalia, would lead to the "development" of a female gender. The same goes for boys. The existence of masculine women and femininities (sporty, tomboyish, butch, drag king, etc.), feminine masculinities (crazy, drag-queen, etc.) proves, however, that the causal relationships between sex and gender (the former causing the latter) or expression (gender expressing sex) have no biological or natural basis. And the Freudian hypothesis of psychic bisexuality or the existence of a "third gender", as it was called in the 19th century, do nothing to change this. Nor does the journalistic chestnut about "gender confusion".

What does this have to do with feminism and its "we"? The type of **sex/gender** model it endorses and which will determine its politics. The type of femininity and masculinity it defends or authorizes. The type of feminist subject it endorses. **Feminism can play the role of guardian of the museum**

of sexual difference. It can also take into account the existence of a multiplicity of genders. It can take advantage of the contributions of gay, lesbian, trans, queer and other subcultures, since they offer different genders and roles, likely to interest all those who do not want to conform to culturally imposed gender norms. Some of these norms are the very ones that have corseted entire generations of women who have been handed the manual of "natural" femininity. But if femininity is no longer the reserved domain of biologically defined women, if it is a cultural construct, if it is mobile, then not only is natural or original femininity a myth, but the production of different femininities is possible. The same applies to the production and transformation of masculinities. And isn't the transformation of masculinity a feminist objective?

THIS PROLIFERATION OF FEMININITIES (MALE FEMININITIES INCLUDED) CONTINUES ONE OF THE OLDEST FUNCTIONS OF FEMINISM: TO reveal the purely social and constructed nature of imposed femininity. To say that the little model femininity serves above all to confine women to thankless or boring tasks, in the name of a non-existent nature. Assigning masculine and feminine roles serves precisely to conceal the extent to which the boundary between masculine and feminine is porous, and this is far from new. Times of war show how society can accommodate this and break down the ban on women's access to so-called "masculine" activities, when the fatherland is in danger.

During the Second World War, in the U.S. and elsewhere, women were recruited by the military industry to rivet shells. The war effort pushed women out of the domestic sphere and out of their conventional roles. *"We can do it!"* proudly proclaims Rosie the Riveter as she rolls up her sleeves to go to work at the factory, on an American propaganda poster that became famous enough to become a fridge magnet or an effigy on a shopping bag. Feminism says it all, claiming for women access to supposedly masculine professions and activities, from aviation to sports, politics, art and intellectual careers. Rosie thumbs her nose at the "feminine condition".

WE CAN DO IT !

No wonder she became a feminist icon remembered by Christine Aguilera and Pink. Skyboys had to reckon with Rosies for a long time to come. When the men returned from the front, the women, who had built up their biceps and tasted the joys of paid work and independence, had no desire to return home and put on the housewife's dress again. The *New Look*, invented as early as 1947 by Christian Dior to remedy the risk of masculinizing women, by imposing the return of the wasp waist and small shoulders, is quite revealing of the kind of anxiety aroused by women's free exercise of gender.

THE SCENARIO OF GENDER PROLIFERATION REDISTRIBUTES THE CARDS. It invites personal and political exploration, experiments in subjectivation and questioning, reminiscent of second-wave feminism and concerning everyone. By taking into account a multiplicity of expressions of gender and sexuality, as third-wave feminism does, the vocation of feminism is multiplied. The paradox is significant: the subject and horizon of feminism are no longer "women", they become "women", femininities and masculinities. Their definitions can remain open-ended, making women and femininity processes, points of arrival rather than fixed points of departure. The same goes for man and masculinity. In this configuration, feminism's relationship to THE woman, its "self-evident foundation", is more complex. It deliberately distances itself from any reification of "woman", of "sexual difference", but also from a homogenous, "natural" conception of masculinity. In her *Raise Your Glass* video, Pink combines empowerment and gender mixing, reincarnating Rosie. The nuts and bolts of the genre have snapped. Rosie knows this, and you won't get her to change out of her plaid shirt and into a Chanel suit.

2.
But what do they want?
Scenarios

FEMINISM BECOMES A COLLECTIVE MOBILIZATION. The fight to reduce inequalities between men and women shifted up a gear and entered the public arena. Feminism took to the streets. In England, the suffragettes organized demonstrations and civil disobedience actions on a par with Act Up. Voluntary arrests, hunger strikes, tax strikes: nothing could stop them. Some lost their lives. On the agenda: access to education, property ownership, voting and employment. All rights denied to women by the Declaration of 1789, which made them "passive" citizens in the text, on a par with children and foreigners.

Dis-moi Emmeline on s'est pas trompées d'époque ?
ACT UP

The feminism of rights is becoming one of the red threads of feminism. It's a **reformist feminism**, often **liberal,** even individualistic. Its demands are sectoral and do not call society into question in a systemic way. This is not the case with the Women's Liberation Movement (*Women's Lib* in the U.S., MLF in France), which is the source and product of major social change.

A social and political movement, the Women's Liberation Movement of the Seventies was part of the great international mobilizations of the Sixties: the Civil Rights Movement in the USA, the anti-Vietnam War pacifist movement and the student movements. It was also born out of the Left's unfortunate habit of marginalizing women by relegating them to menial political tasks or postponing their demands. Revolution first, feminism later. Yes, but when?

THE MLF IS THEREFORE BROADER IN SCOPE THAN REFORMIST FEMINISM. In part, it relays the rights agenda, but without neglecting another equally important objective: the advent of different feminine lives because they are feminist. The movement has developed

WOMEN'S LIBERATION
IS
THE REVOLUTION!!

a precise politicization technique: *"consciousness raising"*. We meet in women's groups to put this famous consciousness-raising into practice, to translate women's "personal" experience collectively and politically. All the more so as, once the trigger has been pulled, it's complicated. The world will never be the same again, and not necessarily more welcoming. Consciousness-raising goes hand in hand with another slogan: "The personal, or the private, is political". Marriage, domestic work and sexuality are not just private matters. They are linked to institutions and forms of social organization that fuel the oppression of women: the state, the family, the division of labor, the control of reproduction. But how can we understand this if we remain isolated and think that our problems are personal or boil down to individual conflicts? Feminism has the answer: by creating links of solidarity between women, deciphering the systemic nature of their oppression and organizing themselves.

Feminism generates its own theory, a critical analysis of patriarchy as a system, but also tools for transforming society and living in it as a feminist.

Launched in the late sixties by members of the *New York Radical Women, consciousness raising* groups attracted over a hundred thousand women in the seventies in the USA alone.

ANOTHER MAJOR NEW FEATURE OF SECOND-WAVE FEMINISM WAS THE ENTRY OF THE FEMALE BODY AND SEXUALITY ONTO THE SCENE. **We tend to forget it today, but the Women's Movement was also, and above all, a movement for sexual liberation.** The body and sexuality were not simply perceived as sources of oppression. They were invested as formidable opportunities for autonomy, experimentation and liberation. Women's emancipation is not simply a legislative crusade to win rights to control reproduction (abortion and contraception). Women need to break out of their social and cultural alienation: they need to be ashamed of having an abortion, of not being a mother, of being single, but also of loving sex. To do this, they need to change and put an end to a whole series of internalized prohibitions. Feminism is far from being reduced to negative criticism and the whining of the "un-fucked", as its opponents call it. It also militates for a euphoric femininity that is no longer passive in all areas. Women must be transformed from objects into subjects. She can and must increase her power to act (*empowerment*), including in sexual matters. Like privacy and culture, sex is political. **The adventure of feminism is nothing less than a radical, collective and subjective social transformation, which goes far beyond the framework of rights and demands for equality.**

Like all major political movements of the nineteenth and twentieth centuries, feminism was influenced by the main currents of thought that ran through them. It also adapted, inflected and criticized them. **Radical feminism** drew its inspiration from Marxism, while pointing out its limitations. Doesn't Marxism prioritize class struggle to the detriment of the struggle of the female class against the male class? For **materialist feminists**, Marxist utopianism and the dialectical resolution of the conflict between the working class and the bourgeois class must be transposed to the level of "sex classes" (the class of men versus the class of women), leading to the abolition of their antagonism. In France, the focus is more on labor and capitalism, at the expense of cultural relays (high and low culture, popular culture, everyday practices), which are less neglected in Anglo-Saxon countries. The Marxist or materialist feminist miracle having failed to materialize, materialist feminism will continue its critique of capitalism, with anarchist or separatist variants, within the framework of informal self-managed organizations.

In the 1990s, **post-structuralism** reinforced socio-constructivist conceptions of gender (femininity and masculinity) by adding a strong discursive dimension: **gender is no longer simply a social construct opposed to "natural" biological sex. Genders and sexes become discursive or performative constructions that are abusively naturalized.** To flush them out, we need to expose how they work. To overcome them, we need to confront them with alternative gender practices. It's no longer enough to say that genres are constructed.

We need to show how these constructions are not made of reinforced concrete, how they are fallible.

New forms of action and new paradigms are emerging. **What's the difference between proper femininity and drag-queen femininity?** A provocative question with a disarming answer that every woman who spends hours getting ready for a party or a wedding knows by heart: heel height, a difference of degree, not of kind. A matter of ritual and repetition. Normative genders need this staging to exist and impose themselves. We spend all our time "performing" gender as it should be. There's nothing natural about that. It's no coincidence that the gender fucking[2] of the nineties comes straight out of lesbian feminist theory and is being lived out at the same time, on a daily basis, in gay, lesbian and queer cultures. It's no longer a question of internalizing gender norms or conforming to them out of calculation or to survive, but of providing the keys to deconstructing them. Instructive for all.

---

2. Literally, the practice of "screwing" your gender.

The scenario of gender proliferation is different from the **abolitionist** scenario of materialist feminism and equality feminism. For these two currents, the goal is to abolish gender, whether they designate gendered classes as forms of capitalist exploitation or marks that will disappear with the advent of real equality. Marxist or not, the abolitionist horizon is a classic of the French universalist tradition, long predating nineteenth-century feminism. On the flip side: rights for all. We're still waiting, and we know full well that women weren't part of the 1789 program, constitutionally speaking. "Progress is being made", we're told. "It'll happen," say the advocates of the policy of small steps. "Enough with the Penelopes," say others. Waiting is part of a predetermined game. **On the plus side, the democracy born of the French Revolution runs on exceptions. It's in its DNA. Universalism rhymes with exceptionalism.**

ABOLITIONISM IS A FORM OF POLITICO-SEXUAL IMAGINARY THAT SCAFFOLDS BY SUPPRESSION RATHER THAN ACCUMULATION. But is eliminating the problem the

ÉGALITÉ
HOMME FEMME

solution? The proliferative scenario, on the other hand, relies on a non-hierarchical, uncontrolled jostling between expressions of gender, some of which are already here and others yet to come. From this perspective, it's not a question of eradicating genres, but of transforming them, adding rather than subtracting. So, the guillotine or the **gender revolution**? **Gender fuck** or a neutral world, if that's even possible? The sad gender **or the extension of the realm of gender**? The deletion of the "1" and "2" on the carte vitale? Yes, but what for? "To go back to zero", say equality feminists. "To go to "10" and more if necessary, because "1" and "2" are not enough," say queer feminists.

CRITICIZED FOR ITS FAILURE TO TAKE MATERIAL AND ECONOMIC REALITIES INTO ACCOUNT, THIRD-WAVE FEMINISM, of which queer feminism is an offshoot, proposes scenarios that focus more on **resistance to gender norms and micro-politics than solely on denouncing male oppression and domination.** In this, he joins the family of affirmative, non-victimizing feminisms. This change of perspective is not due to chance or a tendency towards optimism. It is a function of a different conception of power. Since the modern era, power is no longer exercised solely from classic institutional sites such as the state and the law, nor from a single location, nor in a vertical manner. It is also exercised through a myriad of practices, knowledge and meanings. It increasingly invests bodies and life (what we call "biopolitics"). As a result, the sources of resistance must also multiply, to counter not compact oppression but decentralized power. This is why feminist cultural studies pay particular attention to phenomena of bodily and cultural resistance, tracking them down in the media, art, history, philosophy, psychoanalysis, literature, popular culture and everyday practices.

The idea of a feminist policy based on taking differences into account was gaining ground in the 1990s. Whether sexual, ethnic or "geocultural", these differences are social, not psychological or biologizing. The politics of difference has nothing to do with French differentialist feminism, imbued with Freudian and Lacanian psychoanalysis, which concludes that women and women-mothers are radically and ontologically othereous. This current has refused to be identified as feminist by claiming the constitution of a "science of women", "feminology", and has hindered the feminist project far more than it has served it. **The politics of difference poses a challenge** not only to this current, but also to **universalist feminism and equality feminism,** both of which are reluctant to take into account differences that are perceived only as threatening particularisms.

3.

Sex, Pornography and Prostitution

Sex = power. Sexuality as a space of power and struggle is central to feminism. We could even say that feminism invented sexual politics by taking an interest in the way in which sex is traversed by relations of power, and by trying to remedy them. Feminism has exploded the definition of sexuality. It will never again be reduced to what happens in the bedroom or to the sexual act.

FEMINISM BECAME A SEXUAL LIBERATION MOVEMENT IN THE 1970s. The first wave tended to approach sexuality from a moralistic and hygienist angle: it was not yet personal and political. If sexuality crystallized women's oppression, it had to be criticized for its alienating uses, but also reclaimed and reappropriated. **Sex is central to this struggle. It becomes one of the feminist weapons par excellence** in the challenge to phallic sexuality and the search for a different way of experiencing the body. Criticism and denunciation were accompanied by a veritable sexual fervor, exploratory and playful, whose aim was to rediscover and transform sexuality. Criticism of patriarchy generates an alternative cartography of the female body and pleasures. Workshops are dedicated to the practice of masturbation and **the rediscovery of the clitoris,** to counter "the great penetration" and **"the myth of vaginal orgasm"**, or to valorize **the G-spot (the "female prostate")** as a female cavernous body. The "degenitalization" of sexuality is intended to put an end to purely coital sex, to sexual reproduction and its links with capitalism. Lesbianism becomes the practice of feminist theory, because it allows us to escape heterosexual culture and find ourselves among women. **With rare exceptions, this affirmative and creative politics of pleasure has gradually disappeared from today's movement**, giving way only to

JE NE SAIS PAS
DEMANDE A TON PÉRE
DIS MAMAN
C'EST QUOI
UN ORGASME ?

negative critiques of sexuality and a focus on sexual violence.

THE FIGHT AGAINST RAPE AND CAMPAIGNS AGAINST PORNOGRAPHY MOBILIZED PEOPLE FROM THE LATE 1970S ONWARDS, but it wasn't until the mid-1980s that the war against lesbian S&M and then against pornography took a radical and divisive turn. **The sex war was declared. Against pornography, but also between feminist currents.** Previously, campaigns against images that degraded women did not necessarily have a sexual basis. This was the case with campaigns against pornography, which systematically equated it with rape: pornography was the theory, rape the practice. Anti-porn feminists organized picket lines in front of porn theaters or peep-shows on New York's 42nd Street, displaying bondage images to denounce porn. Violent or not, a cause-and-effect relationship has been established between pornography and violence against women, even if the link has never been proven in practice. A further step is taken when some feminists assert that pornography is in itself violence against women,

SEX WAR

thus justifying the intervention of the law to ban it, as was the case in two states in the USA, before these legal measures were declared unconstitutional.

This conception of **pornography** has divided and still divides feminists. While few feminists support pornography as a form of representation (since it hardly allows women to identify with or be aroused by it) or as an industry, they are against censorship and the anti-sex nature of the anti-porn movement. In fact, the anti-porn movement focuses solely on the negative aspects of sexuality and dominated sexuality. For **the American feminist sex-positiv movement,** the aim is not so much to claim freedom of expression per se, as to propose **a feminist defense of the right to sexual expression,** and a more complex conception of pornography and explicit sexual representations. To the legal solution that has had the collateral effect of censoring feminist SM erotic publications, and not just misogynist pornography, **why not create a different, feminist pornography?** In response to the sex war, a number of American women directors are starting to produce pornographic films made by women, with some success. **Postporn feminism** took over in the Nineties from France, dreaming of breaking the codes of mainstream pornography. Unexpectedly, in the age of Internet porn, viewers are returning to cinemas to watch porn film festivals.

So the problem isn't pornography itself, but its conservatism in representing sexual practices. "Exoticized" women, "black studs" and their oversized sex are commonplace in mass-market porn, which disseminates well-known racist stereotypes about the supposed bestial "hypersexuality" of people of color and "sluts". As for the anti-porn movement, it perpetuates a binary, essentialized vision of gender (innocent, subordinate women on one side, dominant, violent men on the other), as confirmed by its war against SM and *butch/fem* subcultures in the Nineties, which were equated with guilty male or masculine cultures. In fact, lesbianism is only valid as a feminist political practice if it is synonymous with "sex between two feminine women". Yet this is just one of many combinations in lesbian sexual culture, which includes many forms of feminine masculinity that play a role in sexual attraction. Male lesbians will be accused of collaborating with patriarchy. The eroticization of power in consensual S&M games will be denounced on the grounds that power is essentially masculine. The return of penetrative sex and the arrival of prosthetic sex, with its various metamorphoses and reappropriations of the dildo in the 1990s, were interpreted as betrayal or regression.

The retort of sex-positiv, then pro-sex feminists[3]? Emphasize "consensuality" as the rule in sexual exchanges and games, and remind us that sex is anything but natural. This feminism also emphasizes the empowerment provided by women's appropriation of masculinity, or the production of new forms of masculinities that are non-patriarchal and non-biological, since they are independent of the male body.

---

3. The hexagonal version of the sex-positiv movement, which dates back to 2001.

DU SM SI JE VEUX QUAND JE VEUX
SM SAFE SANE CONSENSUAL

The debate on prostitution has much in common with the debate on pornography. For some feminists, prostitution, like pornography, has become THE violence against women, even rape, considering that the activity of porn actress or prostitute can only be exercised coercively. Exploitation is not just economic. It's also moral: sexual trade, even if consensual, means the **commodification of the body**, which is unacceptable. Moreover, prostitution always has a traumatic origin. It can be explained by sexual violence suffered in childhood (particularly rape), and results in psychological disorders such as "psychic dissociation" or "decorporalization". This medical and psychological discourse "pathologizes" prostitutes and denies them any capacity to act. With regard to paid sexual exchange, they insist on **the continuity that exists between certain types of male/female relationships: marriage and prostitution**, for example, which have in common the provision of financial compensation in exchange for sexual services. They are opposed to all forms of exploitation, economic or otherwise (sex industry and trafficking), and

Pute Power

campaign for independent sex work (without pimps, including the state) and a corresponding status.

Abolitionists, who transcend the right/left divide and the purely feminist sphere, advocate a ban on prostitution that should lead to its disappearance. The state must intervene to punish pimps and clients, and save prostitutes from prostitution. **For sex workers and "whores" (to use their autonomy), who have been organizing since the 1970s** (in the form of movements or unions), the **urgent need is to decriminalize prostitution.** Sex work must be removed from its illegal status, which is the consequence of state regulation of prostitution. Where feminist abolitionists see unambiguous sexual and economic exploitation, for feminist sex workers and whores, it's work that needs to be legally, socially and culturally recognized. The non-recognition of their activity, the lack of status, is at the root of the violence to which prostitutes are subjected, and in particular the daily police harassment. On the other hand, sex workers have specific expertise and feminist and cultural resources that are assets in the fight against forced prostitution, trafficking and abuse in the sex industry, as well as in the fight against HIV. Provided that feminist abolitionists don't speak for them. **Feminism and prostitution are not incompatible**. On the contrary: many sex workers insist that the various activities linked to the sex industry, from sex work to striptease, are significant sources of *empowerment* and sexual affirmation. **"My body belongs to me"** was the famous feminist slogan of the 1970s. It was soon supplemented by the lesser-known slogan *"My ass is mine"*, coined in the early days of the San Francisco whore movement.

4.

Conquering Public Space

France is one of the Western countries where resistance to the presence of women in the public sphere (political, cultural, artistic and intellectual) is strongest. The weight of the universalist republican tradition on French feminism as a whole reinforces the imposition of an abstract, non-real democracy. It goes a long way to explaining this particularism and democratic deficit.

In fact, public space is "gendered": it traditionally belongs to men, who use it for business and politics. Women have been, and still are, assigned to domesticity and privacy. The negative connotation of the expression "public woman" speaks volumes about the fact that public space is

DROIT DE VOTE : 1945
PRÉSIDENTE ÉLUE : ?
QUI VA GARDER LES ENFANTS ?

a place of male privilege. **Access to the professional sphere and political representation therefore crystallized the efforts of feminists right from the first wave.** To symbolize their exclusion from the right to vote, English suffragettes physically occupied public space by chaining themselves to the gates of Parliament at the very beginning of the twentieth century. In 1918, they were partially successful, preceded by New Zealand and Australia, which granted women the right to vote and to hold political office in 1893 and 1895 respectively. The United States followed in 1919, but **it wasn't until 1945 that women were able to vote in France.** The problem was that the right to vote did not resolve the issue of the composition of political staff, which remained predominantly male.

FROM 1945 ONWARDS, THE FEMINISM OF GENDER EQUALITY AND WOMEN'S RIGHTS BECAME INTERNATIONALIZED AND INSTITUTIONALIZED through bodies such as the UN, followed by Europe, with the Council of Europe. **A new political register has emerged: that of the fight against discrimination against**

women, which requires the implementation of tools, such as **positive action**, to put an end to both formal equality and real inequalities. From now on, these inequalities will be observed and measured, with the introduction of statistics and best practices. States are encouraged to introduce legislation and preferential measures to guarantee gender equality. **Some of the French feminists who emerged from the MLF evolved in their relationship with the practice of institutional power and state feminism**. They swelled the ranks of reformist feminism, which saw legal means as levers for change. As we know, French universalist culture is allergic to all forms of temporary affirmative or corrective action, as they are perceived as undermining the principle of equality based on the undifferentiated treatment of individuals. Feminists therefore opt for a French adaptation of the notion of **"parité"** to remedy the under-representation of women in political staff. Intended to avoid the accusation of introducing quotas or "Anglo-Saxon-style positive discrimination" measures, the parity strategy nevertheless

MISS
POTICHE
LA PLACE DES FEMMES EN POLITIQUE

failed to solve the problem: **in 2012, France was lagging behind, and all political parties preferred to pay the financial penalties that apply in the event of non-compliance with the parity law passed in 2002.**

Like all feminist scenarios, that of parity implies a definition and a role for sexual difference. The work of feminist historians has shown that abstract universalism actually corresponds to masculine universalism, and that **the exclusion of women from the public sphere since the French Revolution is neither an accident nor a prejudice, but an integral part of the democratic functioning that emerged from the Enlightenment.** The idea of reformist parity feminists is to remedy this chronic dysfunction, by making parity a principle of access to an enhanced form of equality, which would make it possible to achieve total equality by including the other half of the world, namely women. Only this reintegration would make it possible to achieve the true universal, one that takes into account the gendered dimension of humanity and then transcends it in an ideal, neutral equality. With this conception of equality and sexual difference, parity acquires a transcendental, foundational and timeless value, rather than being a mere tool. The problem is not only that it has not proved its effectiveness, but also that this conception of ultimate democracy carries within it the exclusionary potential it denounces. It imposes the political primacy of sexual difference as a source of social inequality, and a "naturalizing", binary model that exceeds real gender. This primacy of sexual difference as the primary source of inequality is all the more questionable in that it introduces a de facto hierarchy between forms of oppression (compared to "racialization", for example).

In its absolutist version, **parity articulated around the sole axis of sexual difference thus revives a form of democratic exceptionalism.** Its renewal of universalism is incomplete, and fails to take into account the other forgotten aspects of modern democracy: the poor, racialized and/or sexual minorities. This strategy has also instituted

C'EST COMPLET.
MADAME
MONSIEUR
MADAME
PARITÉ VS DIVERSITÉ

a sequencing in political action. By proposing a minimalist version of parity with only two terms, in which women come first, whereas parity in itself is not necessarily binary and can be conceived in several terms and on a cultural level. In a universalist, anti-multiculturalist country, this sequencing and form of parity are in direct conflict with current demands for "diversity", which are far from being a male-only concern. In addition to their effectiveness, affirmative action measures are more flexible in time, and favor concomitant rather than competing actions aimed at those excluded from the public sphere. They do not need to be enshrined in the marble of the Constitution, which is no guarantee of real social transformation and political representation. **So, French-style parity: a false friend of equality?**

5.

Women's Cultures, Feminist Cultures?

Is there such a thing as women's culture? Has it been prevented? Or does it exist, but has been rendered invisible or not recognized as such? The status of writer, for example, was long reserved for men, while women were branded "sentimental scribblers" as soon as they dared to aspire to a literary career. But it all depends on the definition of culture and the strategies adopted. If culture rhymes with high culture and aesthetics (the noble arts), and second-wave feminism's observation that women's culture takes place within patriarchy, how can we escape it? **How can we be sure of forging or recovering women's cultures that are not determined by the dominant male culture? Is**

UNE CHAMBRE À MOI,
C'EST DÉJÀ ÇA.
VIRGINIA WOOLF

there, in the past as in the present, an outside of patriarchal culture likely to be invested by different feminine practices? The answer from **differentialist feminism** is "yes", based on its definition of woman as radically different from man in biological and/or psychic terms. As a result, her writing is different in form and content. Reconnected to her feminine self, to her differentiating maternal function, to a pre-symbolic and impulsive stage, the writer finds the path to her own creativity.

The seventies and eighties saw the emergence of literature and artistic claims that celebrated women's irreducible femininity, such as the French **"feminine writing"** of Hélène Cixous. Thanks to Freud and Lacan, the "phallogocentric" functioning of language was denounced. We advocate an authentically feminine, experimental form of writing that values the evocation of feminine bodily flows and an anti-oedipal narrative syntactic destructuring. The limit of this strategy, apart from its elitism, is to lead to a "renaturalizing", not to say essentialist, vision of femininity; to advocate the purity of literary subversion and an anhistorical, universalist conception of woman, dependent on a fixed, binary and biological definition of gender difference.

A broader, more sociological definition of culture leads to more complex, less heroic and less elitist realities. Popular culture and the practices of everyday life - in a word, the way of life and referential universe of a group, its relationship to the "us" of class, race, history and nation - are an integral part of culture. The question, then, is to understand **how women and feminists, like other subordinated cultures, do or do not act in resistance.** This is because one of the characteristics of feminism is its problematic relationship with dominant or imposed femininity, which is an offshoot of the patriarchal system. The main enemy of feminism, even if it's hardly ever stressed, particularly in feminisms that rely on intrinsic forms of solidarity between women (*"**Sisterhood is powerful**"*, as we used to say in the Seventies: "Sorority is our strength"), isn't it also women who are resistant to feminism, or women who embrace the alienating forms of femininity dispensed by women's magazines?

Feminists emphasize what unites them politically, and are reluctant to evoke their divisions for the sake of efficiency. At the same time, feminism must confront its contradictions, variations and genealogy. Historical studies and the work of Anglo-Saxon culturalists nuance the division between female alienation and feminist resistance. Cultures of femininity in the seventeenth and eighteenth centuries, for example, did not just bring together groups of women overdetermined by their condition, whether domestic or working-class. Women are far from forming a homogeneous whole, with passive subjects on the one hand and economically and culturally active men on the other. Their forms of resistance do not coincide with the standards of twentieth-century feminist ideology. We must therefore take into account a broader and more ambiguous repertoire of modes of resistance.

The same is true when it comes to modes of resistance in the form of **oppositional** or compensatory **readings** deployed by women who consume popular culture. Thus, fans of TV *soaps* or romance novels are not cultural dupes, any more than are teenage girls who invest in **Madonna as a female figure because she is empowering.** Fans of *Star Trek*, for example, have had the show's scripts modified to make female roles more autonomous or less stereotyped.

Without falling into populism or the "romanticization" of these forms of feminine resistance, this cultural non-passivity shows that **feminist consciousness is not the only form of feminist protest.** It may even be useful to break away from the linear storytelling inherited from the Enlightenment (so oblivious to women), which would have us move inexorably towards an improvement in the status of women or the liberation of women. With the idea that it's women from the bourgeois classes and the most idle who have been at the origin of feminism since the eighteenth century. In the United States, for example, the culture of feminist struggle was transmitted by black women to white bourgeois feminists, who did not hesitate to sacrifice the black vote in their battle for the right to vote. There's no denying that contemporary feminism has equipped

Papa don't preach
MADONNA

itself with weapons for the subjective and cultural production of an original and powerful feminist and collective consciousness. But it deprives itself of its basic resources and questioning if it hierarchizes and valorizes only certain militant and recognized forms and figures of feminist resistance. How can we be feminists, and why aren't some women? After all, isn't **the real question that plagues feminism, like all political thought and movements, that of alienation and voluntary servitude?**

6.
Politics of representation I:
The Media

THE QUESTION OF REPRESENTATION IS NOT LIMITED TO POLITICAL REPRESENTATION. Women are also represented in literature, the media, cinema and advertising. The oppression of women is expressed in economic and cultural terms. The production and dissemination of **stereotyped representations of femininity** maintain the patriarchal system or male domination by imposing them as natural. Passive, hysterical, obsessed with shopping or fashion, it's also a double standard that applies when women enjoy sex: "sluts" or "whores", unlike men. **Women are also oppressed through images. Second-wave feminism and Anglo-**

Saxon feminism are well aware of this, and have multiplied their strategies in terms of the politics of representation.

The focus is on content. By highlighting the cultural and constructed nature of negative or stereotyped representations, we hope to trigger awareness and change. The challenge is also to encourage the production and circulation of different images, showing strong women, and proposing **model roles (from Marie Curie to Sojourner Truth, via Wonder Woman armed with a speculum).** Or to overturn stigmatizing names. **"Call me Bitch instead of Madame"** is the title of a famous feminist magazine. Or **"Amazon", "Witch" or "Virago".** In the Seventies, far from being superficial redefinitions, these designations challenged the dominant culture and referred to drastic and utopian changes in life: women left their husbands and careers, experimented with community life and new forms of sexuality, and set about becoming independent, asserting themselves and living differently. Feminism is a counter-culture in its own right.

Wonder Woman
HÉROÏNE CYBORG
TIARE MAGIQUE :
BOOMERANG MORTEL
BRACELETS INDESTRUCTIBLES :
POUVANT RÉSISTER
À N'IMPORTE
QUELLE ATTAQUE
LASSO DE LA VÉRITÉ :
DÉTECTEUR DE MENSONGES
SANDALES D'HERMÈS :
LUI PERMETTENT DE VOLER

IN THIS BATTLE, THE MEDIA ARE THE FOCUS OF PARTI-
CULAR ATTENTION. The first actions were taken against newspapers to challenge sexist advertising, but also to question their editorial content and the male composition of their editorial teams. Wild sticker campaigns on billboards and in public places denounced or hijacked sexist representations. This kind of pressure produced results in some countries, and encouraged the hiring of female reporters and journalists in the mainstream press. At the same time, international women's film festivals were being set up for women, providing essential relays. With the development of feminist theory and cinema analysis (*film studies* and *gender studies*), **cinema came to be seen as a discourse that went far beyond the question of stereotypes and the debate on positive and negative images of women.**

This is because **the question of the influence of sexist images and strategies to combat them is more complex**. How can we achieve products that represent the diversity of women's experiences?

style
VU
à la télé
bra
fashion
shoes

Is this possible? If there are images that misrepresent women, what is the conscious and unconscious part played by men in these productions? And how can we explain their persistence and the power they continue to exert, or even the fascination or pleasure they procure even when demystified, including on female audiences? To what extent do they play a part in shaping male and female gender identities? This also raises the whole issue of reception, since the transmission of the filmic message is not based on a simplistic linear communication scheme, but generates a number of readings.

Film studies proposes answers to these questions and strategies for renewing cinematic language. It shifted the questioning of representation. It's no longer a question of knowing whether or not films are a faithful reflection of women's social reality. We need to approach them as discourses, texts that structure ways of seeing presented as universal, natural or neutral, when in fact they are the result of power relationships that run through our society. Feminist critics and theorists have mobilized a whole panoply of theoretical tools, from Marxism to semiotics to psychoanalysis, in an attempt to grasp how films work. Psychoanalytic analysis of the spectator's position and the limited repertoire of identifications available to her gave new meaning to the goal of turning women from objects into subjects of representation. **Cinema imposes a patriarchal structure in which the woman is the object of gaze for both the film's male hero and the director.** Her body is fetishized, like Sternberg's fixed shots of **Marlene Dietrich's face and legs**. The man alone drives the narrative and the action forward. All the visual pleasure is constructed by a male transmitter for a male audience. **In this configuration, women can never identify with what they see on screen.**

To break out of this ideological and narrative straitjacket, many feminist filmmakers opted for an experimental cinema that would not be tainted by the forms of traditional cinema. The drawback is that the aridity and refusal of figuration characteristic of this type of cinema hardly allow for pleasures in

DIRECTOR'S CUT
THE
CHAIN SAW
GIRL
VERSION
REMASTERISÉE
DVD
VIDEO

reception or alternative identifications. What's more, the analysis and denunciation of patriarchal cinema doesn't work for all films, even in Hollywood cinema and *a fortiori* in other film genres. Other feminist critics have shown how, against all the odds, slasher films (the *Texas Chainsaw Massacre*, for example) are full of surprises. There's the recurring motif of the final girl who always wins in the end. American B-movies, however macho they may be, also feature feminist motifs that are a source of empowerment, even though they are mostly made by men (rape and revenge movies like *I Spit on Your Grave*). This highly structural conception of the male gaze (the patriarchal male gaze) projects the spectator's position, but fails to take into account the empirical reality of reception, as culturalist analyses of cinema have shown.

Many female figures on screen are not, or no longer, passive, and the spectators' registers of identification are both more complex and more unexpected. Indeed, they do not revolve solely around the axis of biologically defined sexual diffe-rence. Women and men can practice cross-gender identifications, identifying with a male character for a woman, for example, and the schematization of patriarchal cinema doesn't take into account other parameters that come into play in identification: race and class. This type of cinema is aimed at white women and focuses on sexual difference. Its blind spots are lesbians and gays, but also black women and men, who do not have the same relationship with the aforementioned male gaze.

The media battle is far from won. It promises to be more difficult than expected, and to require progress on several fronts, without ever being content to be reactive.

7.

Politics of representation II: Art and Feminism

In the countries, places and interstices where affirmative feminism was able to develop, it left its mark on the second half of the 20th century, impacting society, institutions and art. Recent exhibitions have been devoted to feminist art. Their stated missions, their scenography and their vocation to be a living archive contrast with France's timid questioning of women artists, or women artists whom the universality of their art would preserve from any particularism. **Feminist art is inseparable from a form of activism** that can be explained by its starting point: the absence of women in the art world and their overwhelming

(D'APRÈS ROBERT MAPPLETHORPE)

presence as objects of representation according to masculine codes, of which the nude is but one of many examples. From this point of view, for feminist art, traditional artistic manifestations deserve to be invested, and they will be (in painting or sculpture, for example), as do the major artistic currents (body art, environmental art, installation, conceptual art). But they are no more important than art criticism, the occupation of a public space, a fanzine, a ***riot grrrl*** concert[4] or videos.

The scope of feminist art is immense. It consists in distancing itself from readings and images of women and femininity *in* all media. Whether this means investing in representations that remedy the **"invisibilization"** of whole swathes of the reality of **female experience,** or accommodating, in a postmodern perspective, the non-existence of an original and the superiority of copies. **The mass media are a mine of stereotypes, perhaps one**

---

4. Alternative punk rock movement formed in reaction to punk's machismo and anti-feminism.

of the most visible and important sources of objectification and fetishization of women and their bodies.

This is why feminist art has seized on fashion photos, advertising, erotic or pornographic representations and films to criticize them by hijacking them, denouncing them, reappropriating them, or revealing their unnatural, restrictive or oppressive character. From this point of view, it quickly becomes clear that **femininity is a masquerade, a coded performance whose effectiveness lies in its repetitive nature, which can be turned on its head** by means of "decontextualization" and reappropriation, thus exposing its constructed nature. This is one of the reasons why performance art as an art form was so prominent in feminist art from the 1970s to the end of the 20th century.

PERFORMANCE ART IS ONE OF THOSE ART FORMS THAT DOES NOT BELONG TO THE REALM OF HIGH ART. Proportionally, this is of less interest to feminist artists, apart from a few forays into experimental film or video and abstract art. **Performance art is as well suited to**

feminist expression as it is to other minority artistic approaches. It is conducive to blurring the boundaries between **private and public, art and politics, art and everyday life.** Whether it's happening or action, it allows us to explore the famous link between the personal and the political, with a few reorientations. For example, when it takes its inspiration from **consciousness-raising** groups. It's a concern that hardly preoccupied male performers who mistook women for paintbrushes, like Klein and his blue anthropometries. The other advantage of performance art is that it allows us to extract ourselves from any narrative, whether novelistic or theatrical, and even to work without a fixed or original text. Above all, it can be carried out at low cost, which is important if artistic practice is to fulfill its vocation of enabling as many people as possible to rework everyday life, or even to remove the boundary between art and life.

It's no coincidence that **some of the most influential feminist works are collective, dealing with domesticity and the body.** Such

is the case for the famous ***Womanhouse*** project[5] developed by Judy Chicago in Los Angeles in 1972, which is exemplary of feminist political and artistic work on the boundary between the private and the public. By redecorating a house from top to bottom, the twenty-four participants in the project offer a double critique of domesticity: through their choice of "decoration", which reinvests feminine and bodily functions, and by transforming a stuffy private space into a public exhibition space where performances are staged on themes of "feminine" life (*waiting, for example*, in Faith Wilding's performance).[6]

With Lacy, Labowitz and Lowe's 1977 performance ***In Mourning and in Rage***[7], art and feminist sexual politics merge. Seventy women dressed in black and one in red demonstrated their anger in front of Los Angeles City Hall to protest the murder of ten women by the Hillside Strangler and the sensationalist media coverage that followed. **The**

---

5. http://womanhouse.refugia.net/

6. http://www.reactfeminism.org/nr1/artists/wilding.html

7. http://www.youtube.com/watch?v=767U43psfn4

art serves to denounce the gendered nature of public space, the fact that, unlike men, women are not safe there. A woman walking alone at night has to ask herself questions or impose restrictions on herself for fear of being attacked. Marches against rape and to reclaim a public space that remains *unsafe* for women - such as **Take Back The Night** and the **Slutwalk** - are directly inspired by this. In this case, it's the repetition of the artistic performance that ensures its durability and feminist transmission. This is all the more precious as it is an ephemeral art form that leaves no traces unless filmed. The other great quality of performance art for feminist art is that it does not exist without interaction with the audience, whether this involves confronting it, reflecting back its own objectifying gaze or connecting it with a minority audience. Finally, performance art favors the staging and use of the body, which is one of the recurring themes of feminist art, marked by an exploration of gender that includes the performance of masculinity. **For all these reasons, performance art has been and remains one of the privileged means of expres-**

sion of feminist art, and not just feminine art. There is little trace of this in the art market or in permanent collections, which display their "great women artists" like so many coat hangers.

8.
Discourse on Method

IN THE WAKE OF THE 1970S, FEMINIST THINKING ATTACKED ALL THE SCIENCES, "the humanities" and "the hard sciences" alike. Women have been excluded from the scientific field, and scientific knowledge about women is produced from a male point of view. But the issue is also epistemological: what role does gender play in the power relations inherent in the construction and validation of scientific knowledge? **The production of knowledge is political from the moment when some of it is disqualified or measured against the yardstick of a conception of objectivity that feminists will set out to deconstruct,** by demonstrating its socially and historically constructed and gendered character.

Ne bougeons plus...
LA FABRIQUE DE L'HYSTÉRIE

This is nothing less than a return to the neutrality of scientific truth.

Theory and the experimental method, with all their validation procedures, and life in the laboratory, are the subject of critical investigations that show that scientific objectivity, as it has been constructed and claimed, is situated and partial knowledge. If it doesn't present itself as such, it's all the better for claiming to be neutral, universal or transcendent. **"True science" is built both on the exclusion of women and on practices that are coded as masculine.** The scientific position of Boyle, for example, the "father" of chemistry and experimental science, is built on a set of gendered oppositions and exclusions: the true scientist is a white man, objective, serious, technical, abstract and transparent. **He is the ventriloquist of the world and of objects. Disembodied, he is on the side of the spirit.** If they are not scientists, women of a certain rank may be worthy of attending public presentations of his famous air pump experiments, but they can never serve as valid scientific

witnesses. The cumulative function of spectator and witness is exclusive to the male part of the audience, according to the procedure for establishing scientific truth invented by Boyle. This is because women are **coded as subjective, ridiculous and concrete. They are on the side of the body, not reason.**

Feminist science studies and technology studies seek to highlight the biases of scientific objectivity and restore the contingency of science as it is actually done. They reassess the division between objectivity and subjectivity, and propose new scenarios for the production and practice of knowledge. **"Feminist objectivity" denounces the false separation between objectivity constructed from a male point of view and politics.** It invites us to take into account the network of "subaltern" actors who participate in the production of truth, be they women or the collective that lies at the root of all scientific endeavour, and which is masked by the individualizing storytelling of "the discovery" and the genius scientist. From a Marxist empiricist perspective, objectivity is perfectible and remains an objective, but it will have to be supplemented to improve it from a feminist point of view. **In the so-called "hard" sciences, as in the humanities, the promotion of situated knowledge calls for greater reflexivity, taking into account the anchoring of all discourse and the importance of point of view.** For some, this means reintegrating marginalized points of view and knowledge, while for others it means giving them preference and the benefits of the partial vision they provide, while avoiding the trap of relativism.

Over the past twenty years, the toolbox of feminist epistemology has been tested and added to. The concerns raised by these new knowledge practices and this type of reflection-action have been allayed. The valorization of situated knowledge has not led to blissful idealism, nor has it exonerated it of all suspicion. Taking minority viewpoints into account has not led to identity or community rigidities. In countries genuinely impacted by the feminist revolution in all its dimensions, including its implications for the politics of knowledge, new research ethics aimed at justice and social transformation have developed. They take into account knowledge presented as "subaltern" or "minority" insofar as it emanates from specific groups ("racialized" minorities, for example), and attempt to reduce the objectifying gesture of researchers, including in the social sciences. *A fortiori,* in research that mobilizes "subjects", the latter are considered not as research objects, but as active partners, full players in any project that consists of producing social theory. The notion of "positionality", which consists in assessing one's privileges and geocultural and political anchorage, is also part of this desire to do "with" and not "on". Lastly, the "politics of the canon" - in other words, questioning the referential universe practiced in places of knowledge, such as universities - have made it possible to stop privileging dominant knowledge and actors to the detriment of others. **Feminist knowledge policies have led to significant epistemological upheavals. Far from limiting themselves to the transmis-**

sion of feminism or feminisms, they propose an interdisciplinary field and a constantly evolving discourse of method, where the feminist perspective is transversal.

sion of feminism or feminisms, they propose an interdisciplinary field and a constantly evolving discourse of method, where the feminist perspective is transversal.

9.

Feminism and Gender

What about the relationship between gender and feminism? It's an interesting question, all the more so as French feminists, who today swear by "le genre" and not "les genres", were the same ones who, ten years ago, saw it as a useless Anglo-Saxon invasion and were irritated that we didn't speak of "de rapports sociaux de sexe" instead. It's true that the mere mention of the term is enough to attract European or national subsidies for research that distances itself from overly political feminism. In Europe's **gender mainstreaming** policies, for example (the integrated approach to gender equality policies), the notion of "gender" is no more than a simple bureaucratic indicator, in line with a traditional definition of gender and sexual difference: "Gender" is synonymous with "man" and "woman".

"Gender theory" has recently appeared in the French media as something new. It has even emerged as a formidable weapon to use against opponents of high school teachings that mention homosexuality, as if gender and sexual orientation were the same thing. Not only is there no single theory of gender, but it is not exclusive to feminism. **The notion of "gender" long predates feminist theorizing.** Anthropologists used it to designate the social construction of masculine and feminine roles as early as the 1940s, followed by psychiatrists and psychologists. Not progressive in itself, it was used to straighten out "effeminate" men and justify questionable surgery on intersex and transsexual people. It's only when feminist theories take hold of it that the notion is considered from a political point of view, and we enter into a frank critique of gender as imposed.

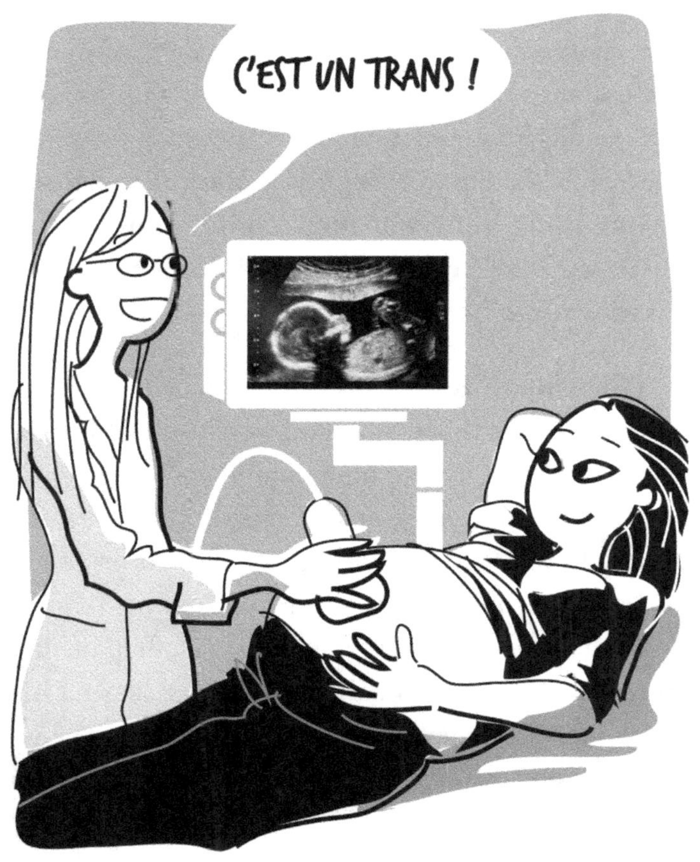
C'EST UN TRANS !

Second-wave feminism focuses on a critique of the normative construction of femininity that confines women to limited gender roles and expressions. It denounces the gender oppressions that result from the asymmetry between "masculine" and "feminine". **When it aims to reduce inequalities between men and women, the term "gender" refers to the biological couple "man/woman".**

Third-wave feminism, in its queer movement, proposes a critique of gender with a different spectrum. Male/female binarism favors an indexing on sexual difference (male/female). It proves too narrow to understand other gender identities, such as feminine masculinities and masculine femininities, masculinities and femininities that do not correspond to the so-called biological sex. **This feminism is always interested in the oppressive effects generated by blocked conceptions of gender, but also in the positive effects generated by the existence and possibility of different genders that resist normative**

models. Gender is seen in relational terms, and the circulation of masculinity and femininity no longer depends on biological sex.

This evolution is due to the fact that **queer feminism** takes into account a multiplicity of genders once (and still today) considered pathological deviances. Third-wave feminism positively embraces different gender identities, particularly those that flourished in the gay, lesbian, trans and queer subcultures of the 1990s, with butch, neobutch, drag-queens and drag kings, transsexuals and transgender people. **Second-wave feminism explores femininity rather than masculinity. Queer feminism works on femininity, but it also ventures into the terrain of masculine production and identifications (male lesbians, FtM[8], MtF[9], heterosexual masculinities). He criticizes normative masculinity in other ways.**

---

8. Trans Female to Male.
9. Trans Male to Female.

BUTCH
FEM

What second-wave feminism and third-wave queer feminism have in common is a desire to break the naturalistic straitjacket of gender indexed by sexual difference, by proposing a critical and political use of gender. **Second-wave feminism seeks to transform the model of dominant femininity. Queer feminism seeks to pluralize "models" of femininity and masculinity.** It seeks to identify and enable new forms of masculinities and sexualities, and thus new bodies and practices. Here again, **the meeting point between these different critical approaches is their anti-naturalist conception of gender and the political gaze they cast on the effects of the dominant sex/gender system.**

With the explosion of university courses dedicated to **women's studies** and **feminist studies** in Anglo-Saxon countries in the 1980s, and the spread of gender as a category of analysis across all disciplines and cultural studies in the 1990s, gender made a dramatic and fruitful entry into critical theory. The late arrival of the notion of "gender" in French

QUEER !

feminism - which had refused to invest the academic field - and its current confinement to a sociology of norms contribute to a devitalization of its critical and political potential. **Examining the weight of "gender norms"**, if not "gender", **contrasts with the interest of feminists and gender studies in forms of resistance to gender**, and in different or alternative genders. **When "gender" simply refers to the difference between "man" and "woman"**, as defined by the international institutions that have imposed gender mainstreaming[10] or the feminist reformism of equal rights, the term once again becomes synonymous with "man" or "woman", and **the gain is nil**. In fact, it contributes to the depoliticization of feminism and the erasure of gender diversity. It also delays the recognition of the malleability and **plasticity of gender, which concerns and may interest everyone, not just sexual and gender minorities.**

---

10. Gender mainstreaming advocates an integrated approach to equality.

The focus on sex and gender as a cultural and social construct very often leads us to forget about sexuality. **In the opinion of some queer theorists, gender should not be the only prism of analysis,** as it does not allow for a satisfactory approach to sexualities. Indeed, the modification of gender as a source of social transformation often overshadows another, namely the emergence of new sexual practices. Such is the case with SM practices, where gender is not a discriminating factor. **Yet feminism quickly abandoned sexuality to focus exclusively on gender oppression (filiation, kinship systems based on the reproduction of the exchange of women, for example) and not on sexualities in their affirmative, non-normative dimension.** Feminists at war with pornography, rape and S&M lost sight of sexual transformation and practiced a "monogenre" feminism (focused solely on women).

Deprived of its feminist and minority roots, and its impact on everyday life, the theoretical and political tool of gender serves more to reify and reinforce

YEAH!

the normative vision of gender than to challenge it. This raises the question of the effects of the institutionalization of feminism and so-called "gender" studies, and of the links between universities, social movements and subcultures. This question is all the more acute in France, where the transmission of feminism has not really taken place.

10.
Feminists, until when?

HOW CAN THE WOMEN'S MOVEMENT CONTINUE? What does the future hold for feminism at a time when its progress may seem slow? At a time when its achievements (the right to abortion and contraception) are being called into question? Hasn't the cause of women been definitively adopted by international bodies such as the UN and Europe, which advocate gender mainstreaming?

In the 19th century, feminism took to the streets. A pack, a hysterical crowd for some; happiness, a collective celebration for others. With gender mainstreaming, feminism has taken to the elevator and perched itself in the offices of international organizations. It is mainly carried out in partnership

LE GENDER MAINSTREAMING

with public authorities and states. **In terms of feminist strategy and agenda, it is the scenario of equal rights feminism that it imposes to the detriment of other currents (radical feminism or socialist feminism, for example)** and at the cost of a serious recalibration of objectives. This redistribution of tasks and of the agenda goes hand in hand with major reorientations: a dilution of feminism in the generalized fight against discrimination, which places it, like other public policies, in the role of protector of the individual; a narrowing of its spectrum of intervention, which now coincides with the fight for rights; the loss of its protest dimension in favor of a reformist positioning.

This scenario favors **victimization** at the expense of **empowerment strategies** and recourse to "microcultural" resources - in a word, feminist culture. In the fight against violence against women, for example, identification as a victim has become a *sine qua non*, as has the intervention of the state, public authorities, civil society and the legal system. **This condition of victim implies an intense "psychologization"**

that serves as both analysis and remedy. Female rape victims in particular are described as "dissociated" or in a "stupor" that ultimately deprives them of any capacity to react or act.

So the question arises: **is the generalization of this agenda progress or a hindrance to feminism?** What degree of complicity does this hyper-institutionalization of feminism have with neoliberal democracy? Especially since it's clear that if the policy of gender mainstreaming is eroding feminism, it's also because it presupposes an *a minima* definition of gender. "Gender" is so much more presentable and less political than the dirty word "feminism". Gender management, like diversity management, has supplanted the plurality of feminist scenarios and gender identities. The arrival of students in university courses specializing in "gender", who wouldn't consider themselves feminists for anything in the world, but who want to pursue careers as "femmocrats", is a clear indication of the gap between feminism and gender mainstreaming.

MINISTÈRE DES DROITS DE LA FEMME
RÉPUBLIQUE FRANÇAISE
Liberté • Égalité • Fraternité
VOUS ÊTES VICTIME ?
CLIQUEZ VICTIME
A l'occasion de la journée
internationale de la femme…

One might even wonder to what extent this gender-integrated managerial management is not part of a form of "postfeminism". In Western countries, **postfeminism signals the end of feminism.** To speak of postfeminism is to say that the demands of the feminists of the seventies and eighties, and in particular equality, have been taken for granted, to be replaced by pro-woman politics. Media-friendly and different from the backlash[11], **postfeminism advocates a return to traditional feminine values that feminism would have deprived these women, who find themselves single and out of step with their "biological clock".** What's more, it's totally compatible with individual management of the problems caused by feminism through self-help or coaching: it's **the "Bridget Jones syndrome".** In the post-feminist era, marriage and motherhood, as well as gossip and domesticity, are once again the main preoccupations of ***desperate housewives*** and the liberated New Yorkers of ***Sex and the City***.

---

11. The antifeminist backlash generated by the success and visibility of feminism.

THE DEVELOPMENT OF TRANSNATIONAL FEMINISM IS A CRITICAL RESPONSE TO THE NATION-STATE FEMINISM OF which gender mainstreaming is the expression. Emerging from the feminisms of *Women of Color*, Third World feminists, multicultural and international feminisms, it proposes a practice conscious of its historical, geographical and political location. This feminism approaches globalization differently from the "feminist" policies defined and put into practice by Euro-America, the West or the North. It aims to **resist the political and intellectual constraints posed by current international feminism**, its tendency to homogenize women's oppression around the world, neglecting colonial and neo-colonial contexts, and to disseminate representations of women in emerging countries as passive victims. Under the pretext of universalism, the feminism of nation-states practices a politics of differences, which it evaluates with criteria and frames of reference external to the countries concerned. Transnational feminism offers knowledge and tools to counter globalizing logics and practices, which are informed by racialization and class, and by the way they redeploy colonial and neo-colonial relations of domination and subordination. **The imposition of the rights model is replaced by the goal of transnational solidarity based on collaborative policies and agendas.** Anchoring ourselves in local feminist activist communities should enable us to interrogate implicit or explicit power relations within feminist action, and to break with an *a priori* knowledge of what might define feminism in a given time and context.

In its reflections, actions and agenda, transnational feminism thus challenges the pivotal role of the nation-state and the nationalist framework of current global feminist politics. It invites us to reconsider the tensions between states and racialized minorities, which are perceived as threats to the national space, while proposing new forms of ethnicity. It allows us to decipher the joint policies of unveiling and promoting the skirt as a symbol of sexual modernity for Arab and Muslim women. To combat the denial of the role played by racialization in the formation of European identity since the 16th

century. Is it legitimate to speak of postcolonial feminism or postcolonialism at all? Wouldn't it be more relevant to question the racism that has shaped our Eurocentric conception of knowledge and modernity? To ask what lies behind the shield of secularism brandished by French feminists? Civilizationism? A form of sexual nationalism? Nourished by an Islamophobia designed to promote the pseudo-exemplarity of our unfeminist sexual democracy against the new sexual "barbarians"? Countering the state and neo-colonial instrumentalization of women's rights is one of the major challenges facing feminism today.

Epilogue

You weren't a feminist. But then, one day, in front of your TV which was showing the "DSK soap opera" over and over again, following a demonstration or tired of having to deal with "the glass ceiling", you became one. Congratulations! You've taken the first step: overcoming the stereotypes that feminists are saddled with: "ugly", "aggressive", "frustrated", "castrating", "anti-mecs", "ill-fucked", "lesbos", and so on. Onward and upward! Problem: you live in France, one of the most viscerally anti-feminist countries in the Western world, and one that's well and truly mated its revolution. The sweet land of seduction where the feminist aisle takes up less than fifty centimetres in bookshops and libraries. Worse still: this little book seems to be saying that official feminism is unravelling all by itself, entangled in its universalism, essentialism and "whiteness". But there is the great adventure of rights and borderless feminism! Except that it has come to sum up feminism, and is becoming a nuisance in its expansionist aims. The technocrats of gender mainstreaming are relocating feminism. The official PS associations (Ni Putes Ni Soumises and "Osez le degré zéro du féminisme") grind out plan-plan equality feminism, which has much more to worry about than the systemic oppression of women and the question of their empowerment. Add to this fake feminism, a marvellous French exception pampered by the quality (especially left-wing) media and women's magazines, where pages for a campaign against female circumcision, an article on Afghan women and ads for Dior mascara sit side by side.

Your story doesn't look good. Especially as it hasn't been passed on to you. Between the universalist mythology of the Enlightenment and the funny French-style post-feminism, it's feminism in all its creativity and radicalism that's gone by the wayside. **Your "personal" has become their politics.**

Your body belongs to them. Their feminism is stuffed with sweeteners. Not so long ago, it was forbidden to be seen, but now it has a right to be seen, since it has become **feminism by suckers**: that of ministers, senators, macho men and women, and politicians who are upset that women's rights are not respected anywhere but in France. As "monocultural" and antifeminist as French society, the University that was blocking us hasn't opened up: it's just changed its strategy. The devitalization of feminism and its non-transmission are assured hand on heart by mandarins who refuse to co-direct a collection in a publishing house with a woman, but frequent the television sets to lecture. A feminist collection is too serious a matter to leave to a woman, and a feminist at that. But there's no fine here, and the mainstream media are not to be outdone, preferring the teacher to the feminist. So your access to the public space...

So, be a feminist and shut up? Not quite. The current dismantling of feminist politics and culture is succeeding because feminists are being replaced by other actors to spread an expansionist project that no longer has much to do with the project of feminist social transformation. Only feminists, through new forms of activism, will roll back this "feminism without feminists", which is nothing more than a neoliberal politics of standardized female identity. Now is the time to revive an affirmative, transnational and non-conformist feminism. **Feminism has never been a quiet river, but rather a road-movie.**

Feminist reference universe

The anonymous members of the movement, the *next-door* feminist, the activists,

Alarcón, Norma

Alexander, M. Jacqui

Anzaldúa, Gloria

Atkinson, Ti-Grace

Bacchetta, Paola

Barrett, Michele

Beauvoir, Simone de

Bitch Manifesto

Brooks, Shiobhan

Burch, Noël

Butler, Josephine

Butler, Judith

Carby, Hazel

Carthonnet, Claire

Chicago, Judy

Clover, Carol

Collin, Françoise

Combahee River Manifesto

Corinne, Tee

Cottingham, Laura

Crenshaw, Kimberlé

Davis, Angela

Dworkin, Andrea

Export, Valie

Faludi, Susan

Fausto-Sterling, Anne Susan

Feinberg, Leslie

Firestone, Shulamith

Fox Keller, Evelyn

Fraisse, Geneviève

Strass (le)

the suffragettes

Tabet, Paola

Take Back the Night

Treut, Monika

Truth, Sojourner

Varikas, Eleni

Wilding, Faith

Wittig, Monique

Wollstonecraft, Mary

Womanhouse Project

Wonder Woman...

Table of contents

Best sellers Max Milo Editions

Hitler's banker, Jean-François Bouchard

Confessions of a forger, Éric Piedoie Le Tiec

The Koran and the flesh, Ludovic-Mohamed Zahed

Governing by fake news, Jacques Baud

Governing by chaos, Collectif

A political history of food, Paul Ariès

Mad in U.S.A.: The ravages of the "American model",
Michel Desmurget

Mondial soccer club geopolitics, Kévin Veyssière

Putin: Game master?, Jacques Braud

Treatise on the three impostors: Moses, Jesus, Muhammad,
The Spirit of Spinoza

TV Lobotomy, Michel Desmurget

www.ingramcontent.com/pod-product-compliance
Lightning Source LLC
LaVergne TN
LVHW051159060726
842526LV00014B/3270